Playing Minecraft:
Story Mode

By Josh Gregory

Published in the United States of America by
Cherry Lake Publishing
Ann Arbor, Michigan
www.cherrylakepublishing.com

Reading Adviser: Marla Conn, Read-Ability
Photo Credits: All images by Josh Gregory

Library of Congress Cataloging-in-Publication Data has been filed and is available
at catalog.loc.gov

Cherry Lake Publishing would like to acknowledge the work of the Partnership for
21st Century Learning. Please visit *www.p21.org* for more information.

Printed in the United States of America
Corporate Graphics

Table of Contents

In regular *Minecraft*, it is up to you to build your own adventure.

Open-Ended Adventure

Millions of people around the world have enjoyed playing *Minecraft*. It's a fun game that allows players to go on endless adventures. You get to explore a huge world and fight monsters. You get to build anything you can think of. But there are no characters or story. Everything is left up to the player's imagination.

Story Mode is filled with colorful characters such as the Order of the Stone.

A New View of the Minecraft World

Have you ever wished *Minecraft* had a fun story to enjoy as you play? *Minecraft: Story Mode* is just the game you're looking for. It features a cast of original characters. They go on an adventure through the *Minecraft* world. Along the way, they meet famous *Minecraft* monsters. They also visit the locations you know from regular *Minecraft*.

Not the Same Game

Minecraft: Story Mode is not actually a mode in *Minecraft*. It is a separate game that stands on its own. This means you will need to buy, rent, or borrow a copy before you can play.

Tapping buttons as they appear on screen will help you complete many actions in *Story Mode*. Here, pressing the Q key as fast as possible will help chop down a tree.

A Different Way to Play

Playing *Minecraft: Story Mode* is a lot different from playing regular *Minecraft*. You won't gather **materials** or build things. You don't explore a huge open world. Instead, you'll talk to characters and solve puzzles. You also get to make decisions about how the story unfolds. Sometimes you have to press buttons quickly to help a character do something.

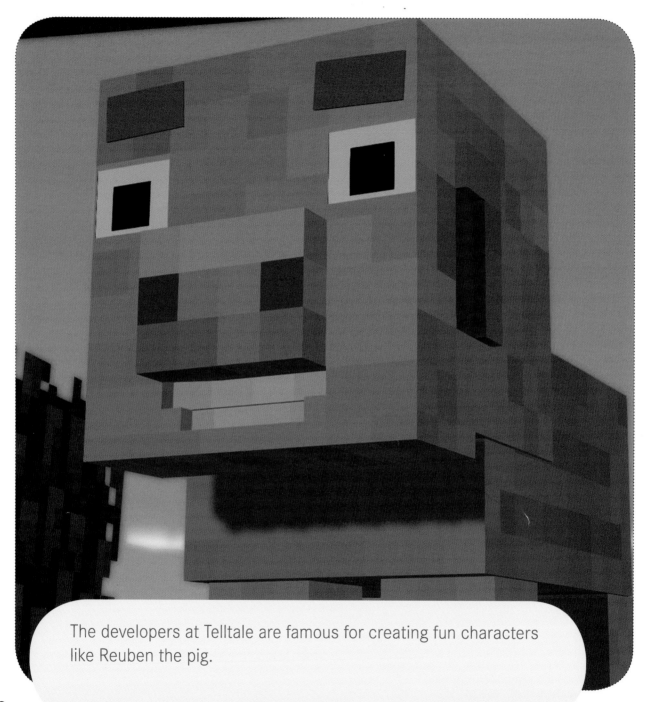

The developers at Telltale are famous for creating fun characters like Reuben the pig.

Telling a Tale

Minecraft: Story Mode was created by a company called Telltale Games. It is famous for creating story games. The **developers** at Telltale were huge fans of the original *Minecraft* game. In 2013, they asked *Minecraft*'s creators if they could make *Story Mode*. Everyone agreed that it was a great idea!

Telltale's Greatest Hits

Telltale has made many games based on famous movies, TV shows, and comic books. Some of them are *Batman*, *Game of Thrones*, and *Guardians of the Galaxy*. Give them a try!

"The Order of the Stone"

Start Episode 1

Several episodes are grouped together into something called a season. So far there have been two seasons of *Minecraft: Story Mode*.

Small Parts of a Big Game

Telltale's games are a little like TV shows. They are divided into small pieces called **episodes**. Each episode takes about an hour or two to finish. The first episode of *Minecraft: Story Mode* was released on October 13, 2015. There have been 13 episodes so far. Fans are still waiting to hear whether more episodes will be created.

Choose Your Appearance

Back

The main character of *Minecraft: Story Mode* is named Jesse.
This name is the same whether you play as a boy or a girl.

Creating a Character

It's time to start a new game of *Story Mode*! The first thing you will do is choose a look for the main character. There are six looks to choose from. Your character's look will not affect the story. The only difference is that boy characters and girl characters have different voices. Pick whichever one you like.

We're the Nether Maniacs!

We're the Dead Enders!

We're the Order of the Pig.

Axel and Olivia are two of the first characters Jesse meets in *Story Mode*. Many others will join the adventure later.

Meeting New Friends

You will meet Jesse's best friends almost right away. One of them is his pet pig, Reuben. Even though he can't talk, Reuben is very funny. Jesse's friend Olivia is very loyal. She doesn't put up with nonsense. Axel is big and goofy. He doesn't always think carefully about what he does.

Famous Voices

Many characters in *Story Mode* are voiced by famous actors. For example, Jesse is voiced by Patton Oswalt if you pick a boy character. Oswalt has acted in everything from *The Goldbergs* to *Ratatouille*. Can you recognize any other famous voices in *Story Mode*?

Talk To

+ Reuben

Try talking to as many characters as you can when you play *Story Mode*.

Time to Explore

Early in the game, you will find yourself in a tree house. Try moving your character around. Look at the different objects in the room. You can pick up some objects and put them in your **inventory**. You will need these items later in the game. Looking for clues and new inventory items is a big part of *Story Mode*. Be sure to inspect each area carefully before moving on.

How about a zombie?

Endermen are cool.

Let's build a creeper!

You have limited time to choose dialogue in *Story Mode*. If the bar at the bottom of the screen runs out, Jesse will stay quiet.

Making Decisions

Another important part of *Story Mode* is making **dialogue** choices. Jesse will chat with many people during the *Story Mode* adventure. You will get to pick what he or she says during these conversations. You might make some characters happy. You might upset others. Your decisions will shape the story. But don't worry about it too much. Just have fun!

Glossary

developers (dih-VEL-uh-purz) people who help make video games

dialogue (DYE-uh-lawg) conversation, especially in a play, movie, **TV** show, or video game

episodes (EP-ih-sohdz) small pieces of a larger story

inventory (IN-vuhn-tor-ee) a display of the items your character is carrying in *Minecraft: Story Mode*

materials (muh-TEER-ee-uhlz) building supplies in *Minecraft*

Find Out More

Books

Milton, Stephanie. *Minecraft Essential Handbook*. New York: Scholastic, 2015.

Milton, Stephanie. *Minecraft: Guide to Exploration*. New York: Del Rey, 2017.

Web Sites

Minecraft

https://minecraft.net/en
At the official *Minecraft* Web site, you can learn more about the game or download a copy of the PC version.

Minecraft Wiki

https://minecraft.gamepedia.com/Minecraft_Wiki
Minecraft's many fans work together to maintain this detailed guide to the game.

Index

About the Author

Josh Gregory is the author of more than 125 books for young readers. He currently lives in Chicago, Illinois.